Strange India!

By
Chakrapani Srinivasa

Strange India!

By Chakrapani Srinivasa

Dedicated to My Dear Parents

About the Author

Chakrapani Srinivasa (Padmaja), Freelance journalist from India possesses Bachelor degree in Engineering (B.E) and Post graduate in Business Management (MBA) with Distinction. He has worked as Associate Editor of 'Naradar' fortnightly journal in Chennai, India. He is the Senior Editor of the journal "The Divineness".

Contributed articles, short stories and travelogues in leading journals like Ananda Vikatan, Kumudam, Savi, Kalki, Dinamani Kadhir, Dinamani daily, Idhayam Pesukirathu, Naradar etc

He has written articles and e books through Smashwords Inc, Kindle Direct Publishing, Atlanta publications, Cooperjal publications (UK), lulu.com, ezinearticles.com, shvoong.com, iproclaim.com (USA).

He is the Consulting Editor: Contemporary Who's Who-Research Board of Advisers of ABI, USA.

Preface

Some strange news and incidents happened in India are exposed in this book.

It will be surprising to know about it.

For example a man is living by eating snakes along the banks of River Gaghra in Bihar. Many more are revealed in this book.

Contents

Poisonous Man!

A man who eats snakes alive!

Niranjan Bhaskar hailing from Ara district in Bihar eats snakes alive.

Niranjan Bhaskar, aged 35, a painter from Bihar State eats snakes daily as his food item.

He says that the snake's blood is sweet and tasty like cow's milk.

He never sleeps without eating a snake.

Daily he will go to the river banks of Ghagra and catch the snakes found along the river and hid between the rocks.

He will chase and catch them alive and he will eat it on the spot itself.

He says "This habit of eating snakes is right from 1977".

—

Poison in Indian Mother's Milk

The presence of DDT has been detected by a research scientist in the samples of mother's milk taken from Chennai, Perungudi, Chidambaram and Parangipettai.

Mother's Milk is a God's gift to all children.

No other food can equalize mother's milk. They are the best, hygienic and safest of all food for children. It has the capacity to oppose all diseases and hence it is given to the new born baby. But poison is found mixed in that very first food given to a human being.

How?

Why?

An investigation was conducted after analyzing the Tamilnadu mother's milk and it was detected that insecticides were found present in it.

Annamalai Subramaniam, a research scientist from Ehinne University has done a thorough study with the support of Toyota Foundation. He has revealed that DDT's presence in Tamilnadu mother's milk.

He has taken 40 samples from Chennai, Perungudi, Chidambaram and Parangipettai and conducted the investigation in a sophisticated lab. He has found out that HCH, DDT and PCB were present in it. When compared to other areas, the Chennai Mother's Milk samples had high presence of HCH.

How can it enter a mother's milk?

In the production, usage and sales of pesticides, India leads other countries. Amongst the Asian countries India stands first and amongst the other nations it holds the 12th place.

Totally 90,000 mt of pesticides are produced in India. 70% of them are used in Indian farms. It is shocking news that most of the pesticides used by us have been banned by foreign countries. DDT has been banned in USA, Hungary, Norway, Germany and UK for a long period. But still it is used in India. 160 countries banned DDT after a meet in Stockholm in 2004. In India to overcome the dangerous mosquito menace we use it still with a special permission.

But till date the mosquito problem has not come down at all. Filarial cases and Malaria cases have increased by 35% in all regions in India.

HCH was banned in India in 1977. To replace it another pesticide LINDANE was recommended. This has all dangerous ingredients like HCH say the experts and environmentalists. When DDT and HCH are used for fields they settle on Vadose Zone. They do not so very easily lose its power. It will take 20 years for DDT to lose its intensity to kill a creature or insect. This gets mixed with water used for irrigation in the field.

Obesity in India!!

In India 11% of the citizens living in metro cities and 3% living in villages are affected by diabetes.

They are all in the age group of 15.

Also it is sad to know that 30% to 40% are not aware that they have excess sugar.

Why Indians are slaves to diabetes?

India has seen famine on several occasions. Due to this a mentality has been developed to cut short our diet. The calories accumulated in our body are not used and converted as fat which is spread all over the body. That's the reason why even a lean Indian has obesity. That's the place where the weight first increases.

Most of this phenomenon is spread from their parents. This deficiency in Indian Women causes defects in Uterus and later on diabetic during maternity period.

Some tips to control diabetics should be known to all Indian Citizens.

To test diabetes certain tests can be undertaken.

Under fasting condition if sugar level is 125 mg/dl or more; under random test if it is 250mg/dl or more then it will reveal that diabetes exists.

These people have very low capacity to release sugar. *TRIGLYCERIDES* will be more than 150mg/dl; HDL Cholesterol will be more than 140mg/dl for men and more than 150mg/dl for women. Blood pressure will also be more than 135/85. One can check these details by themselves and for which a weighing machine and a tape to measure the belly are sufficient.

Our body weight in kg should be divided by double the height of ours. The answer will give the weight index.

This should be 23. But for many Indians it exceeds and that's why obesity is ghastly spreading all over the country. Even the police and army men are affected by obesity and there is a special squad to watch them and warn them.

The percentage difference between the portion above hip and below it should be 1 for men and for women it should be 0.8. By dividing the portion below hip by the portion above hip we get this number. Suppose for a male the portion above the hip is 102cm and for women it is 88cm it shows a signal of danger. For measuring these values you need not go to a specialists or a doctor. Every villager in India can measure it in their homes and huts.

If more than 3 deficiencies are detected then it will reveal that there is a sign for diabetes and obesity say the doctors. After conducting tests in various parts of India it was detected that for those who are more than 15 years age, 40% are affected by diabetes. Are Indians cursed to be affected by diabetes?

Just because the human body opposes insulin, this change in health condition is faced. The food we eat converts as glucose and reaches cell to give calories to our body.

Those who are diabetic have a tendency to oppose the activities of insulin.

So to enable glucose reach the cells, more insulin has to be excreted. But the body fails to excrete insulin and hence diabetes attacks the patient.

To avoid this, every Indian should maintain the 23 as the index number. Daily 30 minutes walk will prevent the forces opposing insulin. It should be a brisk walk. But in India most of the streets have many ups and downs with filth atmosphere. So it does not suit an individual for a free walk. He has to run after parks which are rarely seen in cities. An individual should be able to walk 4km in one hour. Even though this exercise is sufficient; the individual has to see that his intake food does not exceed 1500 calories. If this is not possible then he has to ride on a cycle or swim at least for 20 minutes. Weight lifting and going up and down the staircase will only reshape his structure, but will not reduce sugar level. Instead of reducing the whole body, taking steps to reduce belly is not sufficient. To reduce calories in our diet by 25% most of the Indian housewives and men have the habit of eating food by watching TV and reading books and give strain to their brain. This will increase the calorie values entering our system.

Junk foods can be avoided and fruits and vegetables can be increased. Oil items should be reduced as it will increase the calorie in the food stuff. Most of the oil in India is adulterated. Some brands exhibit that they have sunflower content to reduce cholesterol. Sunola and Saffola are popular in Indian markets. Doctors too advise it in India. Palmolive oil supplied in ration shops reaches the downtrodden at reduced prices.

This will also reduce the fat contents in the fried items. It is sad that frequent reports appear in press that adulterated and duplicate brands are floated in the market. Fake Krishna brand ghee and oil was sold by a greedy merchant in the heart of the city. The original brand is produced in Perundurai in Coimbatore District. Such spurious products are the main reasons for spreading of heart diseases, diabetes and cholesterol in India.

The Pizza culture has also developed rapidly in cities like Chennai and all the youths are slaves to these junk food and chit chat items sold at nook and corner of the city. The dealers usually select the areas near colleges and schools to enhance their business. They do succeed to mint in lakhs of rupees at the same time succeed in making India as an unhealthy nation.

The roadside restaurants which use the third rate and umpteen times fried oil, cater the needs of all laborers and people below poverty line. If idly is sold at Rs10/- piece in hotels, these road side unhealthy shops sell two idlies for Rs.5 or Rs.3 and hence suitable for all poor citizens in India.

The Tamilnadu Government banned these roadside impure stuffs. But still we can see many sprouting all over the city. A leading snacks producing company by name Sowbaghya in Vridachalam sell huge quantity of used oil to these roadside petty restaurants. These merchants have no other go but to purchase this as the fresh oil costs Rs.75 to Rs.100 in the market, which is not affordable for them. This filthy oil is more than sufficient to develop cholesterol and heart patients in India. These petty dealers do their business along the roads which have no drainage facilities. The stagnating water along the road is used for washing the plates and tumblers, which add more diseases to our diseases in our system.

Cricket Stadium for a Son

Yes! Dehrudun is proud to have a cricket stadium in the name of Abimanyu. It was erected by Mr.R.P.Easwaran a Chartered Accountant in Dehrudun. His son Abhimanyu was fond of cricket and so his father initially arranged a cricket pitch near his house and encouraged him to play cricket.

Later on he gradually improved it with his own funds and converted it as cricket academy. He later decided to increase its facilities and also planned to encourage all cricket lovers and youths.

So, he selected a site near Kunniyal in Dehrudun. The entire space was uneven and had hills too. Hence he spent huge sum to level the ground and his move was opposed by the villagers and agriculturalists who owned that land. He had to pay a huge sum as compensation to them and toiled for 4 years to prepare that beautiful 113000sqmt Cricket Stadium.

Even though many rural folks agitated, he courteously and amicably settled the issues and made Abhimanyu Cricket Stadium a memorable gift to his son and youths who were fond of cricket.

What a father!!

What a great work for sports!!

When crores and crores of rupees are rolling in IPL cricket trophy with a great fun and fare a single man has done a marvelous work in Dehrudun in favor of cricket.

Fine!

****

What a Cricket Craze!

I was sitting before a very very busy businessman who was speaking over his cell phone, glued close to his ears. He was hurriedly and pathetically begging to some VIP "Sir! Don't mistake me for asking this! I want a space for at least 2cms!"

"What the hell you are asking for? You want twooooo cms! Oh my God! Simply impossible!" was the reply from the other end.

"Ok sir… sir... Please can you spare at least 1.5 cms?"

"Never!!! Never!!!"

"Please sir .It's my company's prestige issue sir! Shareholders will not tolerate sir! They are even bold enough to bite me to pieces if I don't get a space of at least 1 cm!"

"Hello, there is no point in asking right now. All spaces were booked one year back do you know! What were you doing all these days?"

"Can I get at least 0.75 cms?"

The VIP at the other end coolly said "Ok my friend. I can spare you a space under my left armpit!"

"Oh! Left arm may be objected by our Board. Left means negative signal for them. Can you make it right???"

There was a grave yard silence at the other end, which worried the business man   as he wiped his sweat, which was flowing down like Ganges from his forehead. His eyes and heart shrunk as though he had seen a devil rising from a well. His fingers struggled with his pen on his note pad to note down whatever Gospel poured from the VIP's mouth at the other end.

"Ok 0.25 cms below my arm pit.0.15 cm from right chest!!!"

"Ohhhh! So nice of you sir!!!! It's tremendously generous of you sir to give that great space!!Thank you….. thanks to you sir!!", and the businessman kept the cell down and laughed proudly and heavily as though he has secured a trillion dollar space in Mars!!

I, the extremely puzzled human being sitting before that very busy businessman could not grasp what was happening before my owl like eyes! I have heard about office space, residential space, godown space and our future shattering matrimonial space (apologies to my wife), but I have never heard of a space below an armpit! What the hell space is that to build castle or a workshop!

I keenly asked with a barrel full of curiosity "What's this entire space episode? What for is this heavenly bargain??"

The very busy business man frowned at me and said "You insipid ridiculous creature, where on this earth are you living? You know anything about IPL cricket VVIP super hero players. I am looking for a space in his shirt or pant or cap to display my company logo! You mud pot! Get lost "and he jumped from his cushion seat and ran to the doors to occupy that royal arm pit space of that cricketer!!!

What a cricket craze!!!

_____

_____

Unhealthy Youths

A nations' pride depends upon the working community's welfare.

A nation's economic development is in the hands of youth.

54% of the population in India is male and female youths.

To make a developed nation, their sound health is essential.

Compared to other fields, the youths are more in computer, software, banking, information technology etc. In MNCs they hold key positions. When it is happy to learn about their lucrative salary and perks, it is not satisfactory to know about their health aspects.

Intensive work and less relaxation have made them to fall to prey to BP and heart problems. It is disheartening to know that they are financially sound but health wise weak and sorrowful.

In leading cities like Delhi, Mumbai, Chennai and Bangalore youths forget their normal life and lead an artificial life leading to mental stress and physically burdened. So, in a short period they lose their health and their heart weakens to get various diseases.

Previously heart attack was for the age group 50 to 60. But now even at the young age of 25 many are admitted in hospitals. The main reason is their wrong food habits and culture.

The tendency to consume ancient old healthy foods has disappeared. They feel it to be below their dignity to go after it. Instead they run after fast foods sold at each street corner and sometimes delivered at door step. The restaurants with various dish varieties attract them.

Particularly the fried items, which have low calorific value, are their favorite items. But they fail to know that they fall a prey to disastrous after effects due to it. Pizza and Hamburger have roaring sales in cities.

Chocolates, chips, ice cream, Badam gheer, sweets prepared out of milk cream and cakes are their daily food items. So, very shortly they become stout and awful. This lays the foundation for heart attack very easily.

In India 30% and more are suffering from obesity. This is a big blow to their healthy growth. The hospital statistics say that admission of youths for heart ailment has increased by 15 times when compared to the admissions, which took place 15 years back. 32% of females and 27% of males with obesity problems face deaths due to heart attack.

It is a pitiable figure.

As females feel lazy to cook go after fast food shops and fill their stomach. They are not aware that food items prepared out of preservatives and chemicals leads them to hospitals. Enlightenment to youths about the high salt and Trans fat contents in these items is needed now.

The food stuffs like Parotta, Chapatti, Noodles, Idiyappam and Panneer are sold as instant food items in shops in plastic packets. To avoid decay, the manufacturer mixes several unwanted chemicals, which will spoil the liver. Initially it will cause damages to liver and later on give room for diabetes and obesity. If they continuously eat then they will be affected by heart problems due to mixture of unwanted fats in blood.

Another reason for heart attack for the I.T youths is work load, which results B.P. Especially in IT field they toil day and night. Within a short period they are forced to finish a project and they are subjected to enormous pressure. They somehow manage and execute their duty and achieve targets, which fetches them promotion, incentives and high perks. But eventually in a very short period they are facing blood related problems. Diabetes and liver cancer kills them. One out if ten involved in IT field have some sort of disease. To reduce their mental strain, they need holiday tours, get together with family members and relatives. But they don't do that and run after pubs in week end for enjoyment. Midnight parties are their favorite past time entertainment. At that location they fall a prey to drugs, liquor and Gutka due to bad society. It is worrying information to know that 8 out of every 100 are admitted in hospitals for heart ailment. This is resulted due to unruly weekend enjoyment.

Another aspect, which kills the youths, is the hereditary diseases. In Indians the Lipo protein-A fat is in excess and it spreads to the youths. One out of 4 Indians has this problem. This hardens the blood and affects the blood circulation in our younger generation. That's why Indian youths have poor stamina.

In India there are 10 crore heart patients as per WHO statement. The expenditure to cure them will be Rs15 lakh crore. For a poor country like this it is a monstrous figure and ways to overcome it is not so easy.

The only solution is that the Indians have to change their living habits, says a cardio specialist. According to height they have to monitor their weight. They have to avoid unwanted fatty food stuffs. After consuming fried items in bulk, they sit and do no exercise, which spoils their healthy. Yoga, meditation and morning walk is not followed by all. At least 6 hours rest is needed but they seek refuge in clubs, bars and fast food stalls with a big gang. They don't have the motive to play outdoor games. The companies, which employs them should at least provide indoor games and free yoga sessions.

Cultural shows and entertaining parties should be arranged by the firm to relax them. Many companies fail to do it. They supply fatty items in their restaurants they run inside their complex.

Most of the companies do not conduct routine health check up. Compulsory health camps are needed for the hour. This will help them to realize their disastrous condition of their brain, liver and heart.

All youths should realize that an individual's well being is the prosperity of the society and generation. Death at young age not only spoils the happiness of family, it will kill a country's economy.

It is a national problem in India due to poor environment, culture and food habits. Knowledge and wealth alone is not sufficient for younger generation in India, they need health, which is deteriorating day after day.

Setbacks for Green India

Non-stop smuggling of red rose trees

Eight years back a big committee was formed in Seemandhara to stop the cutting and smuggling of red rose wood trees.

But still that looting is going on.

In south Seemandara we have Chitoor and Cuddappah districts in which we can see Seshachlam with hills like Seshadhri, Neeladhri, Garudathri, Anjanathri, Vrishabathri, Narayanathri and Venkatathri hills.

In Venkatathri hills we have the world richest Tirupati Temple. Several millions visit every year and this hill will be always busy.

Out of 4756sqkm, forest area is 751sqkm. In 2011 it was announced as ESZ area. For transportation 2140sqkm is utilized. So, the smugglers very well use the roads and walk path provided in this hill to smuggle during night hours.

Especially in Seshala hills red sandal wood is cut enormously and hectic business is going on.

Several steps are to be implemented like issue of mobile phones to local tribal men, who form a part and parcel of vigilance committee, rest rooms for forest guard's roads and vehicles for quick approach to interior areas of forests, trained dogs to catch the tree thieves etc. Control by government over the destruction of forests will play a vital role for green India.

Wastage of Water Resources

Chinnakanal and Suruli falls are popular as it contains herbal mix and also caters the needs of unhealthy persons. By taking bath in that herbal waterfall, many diseases get cured. So, these falls in Theni district are big tourist spots. Visitors from Dindigul, Madurai, Virudunagar, and Theni and from north India visit. But they totally spoil by throwing plastic containers and carry bags. They don't realize that it caters the water needs of 50 villages around it. Agriculture is also spoiled by this.

Environmental awareness is poor in rural areas and finally many thousands of acres of lands are destroyed.

In this condition how can our zone become green?

Wrong guidance

Athur farmers have raised a voice that some farmers misguided them by planting coco trees in between coconut trees.

Athur district is famous for coconut trees. Healthy and rich varieties of coconuts were grown to get good profit. In the meanwhile these coconut grove owners were advised to plant coco trees as they can get 5kilo of seeds and it can be sold at Rs160/kilos.

So, believing this statistics many coconut farmers planted coco trees in their farms ion between coconut trees. But unfortunately these coco trees swallowed the growth of coconut trees. These farmers were producing 15000 coconuts but now they could reap only 7000 coconuts. The size also became small and price quoted for it in the market was too low for their survival. The advice given by horticultural experts in Athur has doomed their livelihood.

So, illiteracy and misguidance also has spoiled the green revolution in India.

The growth of Karuvela trees along water resources in Palani district has disturbed the water supply to fields. There are many ponds and water resources in Kanjanayakkanpatti, Erumanayakanpatti and Porulur.

They act as full support for agriculture and domestic needs. But the growth of Karuvela trees along its bank, water is gulped and sucked enormously to drain the ponds,

The steps are to be taken to remove all these dangerous plantations to save water resources, which support green India.

Heroin Dosa!

We have heard of people smoking heroin. But in Vengamedu, Dosa prepared out of heroin is doing brisk business.

Vengamedu in Karur district is like Dharavi in Mumbai. Here we have cheap laborers in large numbers and it is a dirty slum with all evil habits. All cars, buses and trucks passing through Karur after crossing Namakkal, we can see a roadside restaurant. Many low wage workers and tourists throng this restaurant for a special reason.

Their customers will demand Podi Dosa and Pottala Dosa and wait eagerly to taste it. Within few minutes it will be made ready and served hot. Everybody in Tamilnadu is aware of Podi Dosa, which is a common item served in all hotels. But Pottala Dosa is something different. When the shopkeeper tells that name, many will not be aware of its ingredients. A newcomer will blink. But there are regular customers for this Dosa as it is prepared out of heroin.

"This will be, served only to known persons, who will be prepared to pay any amount to enjoy the taste and intoxication. Previously heroin was sprinkled on half boiled egg item. Even in Adai Tiffin item it was sprinkled, as it will be demanded by notorious gangsters. As it will be sour, the customers pleaded the restaurant owner to sprinkle on Dosa item. To intoxicate women travelers, the culprits used this Dosa, says a customer.

A beautiful young lady employee in a textile company says "As a worker in an export company I requested my co-worker to get egg Dosa from a restaurant. He brought it and after eating it, my head rolled down and I fell flat. Many thought that I was sick and fainted. But it was not so. My eyes drooped down and body sunk flat. I felt as though I was flying somewhere. But later on I realized that something unusual ingredient has been mixed with Dosa.

When I asked the co-worker refused to reveal it. As the intoxication was so pleasant I demanded again and again and totally I became an addict to it. Without knowing that heroin is mixed with it I was consuming it daily to have pleasure filled sleep. During that time he had sex with me. For two years I was slave to this and many young girls are trapped by this Dosa! Travelers beware! Be cautious of this dirty Dosa".

Another new method of consuming heroin is that the mischief makers in Velayudampalayam and Thottakurichi areas make a hole on top and bottom of an apple and link these two.

Then they fill heroin on top whole portion and fire it and inhale from bottom portion. Then the heroin juice will m ix with apple and become black. This apple is eaten deliciously by those vagabonds. The sour taste of heroin is changed by apple", says another tourist guide.

****

Mango Murder!!

When summer season sets in, the people anxiously wait for mangoes.

Its sweet taste with yellow skin is loved by all children and aged. Making use of their love and craze, the greedy businessmen have boldly taken a murdering step to mint money in a short spell. They use calcium carbide stones to change its color.

It happened in Madurai, a temple town in Tamilnadu. It is famous for temples and architectural beauty involved in it. But the same Madurai which pleased thousands of Indian and foreign tourists everyday with courtesy and culture now took the toll of many lives by selling poisonous mangoes.

Yanaikal, North Masi Street, North Mada Street and Pudu Street were filled with yellow colored mangoes which were nothing but poisonous mangoes. Though they were yellow in color, when touched it was hard and tough to eat.

Local Administrator Subramanian and Health Officers made a surprise visit to these streets and seized 100 tons of polluted mangos. It worth Rs.1 crore says the reports. Pandian aged 34 living in Pudu Street was arrested along with Palaniandi, the owner of the mango godown.

District Collector Sahayam says "These mangoes are highly poisonous as they are ripened with calcium carbide powder. It will create cancer."

Dr.Sangumani, Government Hospital Specialist said "The naturally ripened mangoes will have vitamin C and are capable of preventing attack of diseases to an individual who consumes it.

But these artificially ripened mangoes will not have this capacity and will create problems in stomach and liver. It will create gas and attack the nervous system and brain. Loss of memory will be a side effect."

Professor in Madurai Agricultural University Kumar and Mariappan say "In a day the green color of the mangoes will be changed to yellow color and they immediately push it to the market for sales. They need not wait for weeks together to ripe it naturally. Only by cutting it we can find out the real one and the poisonous one.

Always buy raw fruits in green color and keep inside a rice drum and after a week it will ripe with yellow color and have good sweet taste."

The Koyambedu market which is famous for wholesale market in Chennai is flooded with chemical mangoes. The dealers here import mangoes from America and Australia. They sell it with mangoes obtained from Andhra Pradesh, Kerala and Maharashtra. After receiving mangoes with international quality they distribute to Pondicherry, Karnataka and A.P. The wholesale dealers sell it to retailers with profit.

In this popular market previously only greenish mangoes which are not ripened will be brought and kept in hay stack to change its green color to yellow color.

But now the trend has changed and due to competition and greediness some new merchants have started the chemical treatment illegally to ripen it in a day. They are happy that they get back their investment in a day instead of waiting for a week. \

Knowing their techniques many mango grove owners send their mangoes in green color in huge quantities to mint money overnight.

The agents who have an agreement with farmers do this chemical hazard. The merchants who used calcium carbide stones now use a sophisticated chemical to change its color. They use the same technique for Oranges, Pineapple, Sappotah, Pappiah, Plantain; Gova etc. 60% of the dealers in Koyambedu are engaged in this dreadful business.

It creates many health hazards. Arumbakkam Sidha Medical Experts says "These chemical mangoes cause allergies, liver wounds, intestine problems, skin problems, itches, burns, boils, etc.

To identify the poisonous fruit we have to soak the mango in a vessel full of water. After sometime that vessel will give out calcium carbide smell, which will tell us that it is nothing but a poisonous one.

Mangoes ripened by using chemical spray are difficult to be identified, because these sprays are manufactured with the flavor of that fruit.

It is a clever mischief done by merchants. It is better to avoid all these fruits now till government takes severe action."

These chemicals are sold in medicine shops at a price of Rs.175/100 ml. Ethipan, Chloro Ethyl Phosphonic acid; Propylene and Chlysol are the ingredients of these chemicals.

To develop farm production these chemicals are used by farmers. It is produced by companies which produce pesticides to kill mosquitoes, cockroaches etc.

It is not advisable to touch it with bare hands and it will create lots of side effects to the person who consumes it.

It should be kept away from children also. Just imagine the bad effects it will create if it is used for ripening fruits like mangoes which are eaten by millions. With 100ml of chemical we can ripen 1.5 to 2 ton mangoes. They mix it with water and spray it liberally for few hours and turn it to yellow color like a magic.

"In foreign countries they have ripening centers. Here color is changed apart from ripening process. In Karnataka the Government has established ripening centre for plantains. In Koyambedu, Asia's biggest market does not have such facilities. That's why merchants use carbide stones and ripen it with greediness" says a merchant in Koyambedu.

Erode District which is famous for textiles and dye factories now is famous for chemical mangoes. In Nethaji market the fruit stalls are receiving mango, Gova fruits in hundreds of Lorries every day.

They will be raw and green in color. It will take 15 days to ripen it. Till such time their business activities will be zero.

Hence to overcome this business loss they use calcium carbide stones inside the mango basket to ripen it quickly. After eating such mangoes many have been admitted in Erode Government Hospitals with complaints like diarrhea, liver disturbance etc. The Health Authorities have warned all the dealers about their mischievous business.

District Health Officer Thangaraj says "I am receiving complaints everyday about this chemical malpractice in mango market. We can see black dots in such mangoes which will tell they are dangerous for health. Intense heat is created artificially and they ripen the mangoes. It causes many side effects and hence food inspectors are posted in all areas to check this dreadful practice."